Dedicated

To

All the Past & Present Judges of the Supreme Court of India.

Salute to their wisdom.

Salute to their interpretation of Law.

Salute to their elaborative judgement writing.

NEGOTIABLE INSTRUMENT ACT- SUPREME COURT'S LEADING CASE LAWS

CASE NOTES- FACTS- FINDINGS OF APEX COURT JUDGES & CITATIONS

JAYPRAKASH BANSILAL SOMANI

Contents

Contents

Preface

Dear Learned Advocates of the Trial Courts, Session Courts, Tribunals, High Courts, Supreme Court, Corporates & Individuals

I am very delighted to provide you a book on 'NEGOTIABLE INSTRUMENT ACT- Supreme Court of India's Leading Case Laws'.

In this book you will get...

1. Name of the Case i. e. Cause title

2.Relevant Sections discussed in the case

3. Hon'ble Judges/Coram of the case

4.Number of PDF Pages in Original Judgement of the case

5. All available Citations of the case

6. Case Note with appeal allowed/ dismissed or disposed off

7. Facts of the case

8. Hon'ble Apex Court's findings, while dismissing/allowing or disposing the appeal

9. Ratio Decidendi if any.

My special thanks to Manupatra, because of their web portal I can compile this book in well manner. I am also thankful to Notion Press to support me to publish & market this book throughout the Country. Thanks to my Juniors, Advocate Colleagues & Insolvency Professional Colleagues to support me in this venture.

Mr Rachit Manchanda has helped me a lot to compile this book.

I hope this book will add some value addition in the wealth of your legal knowledge. Your positive feedbacks will boost me to compile/ write further books & negative feedbacks will improve my skills. Kindly send your valuable feedbacks by email.

Thanks with Regards,

Jayprakash B. Somani

Advocate, Supreme Court of India

Email: jaysomani64@gmail.com

Web Site:www.jayprakashsomani.com

Call: 8384051134, 9322188701, 9318381287

Acknowledgements

Printed & Publised by

Notion Press

No. 8, 3rd Cross Street,

CIT Colony, Mylapore,

Chennai, Tamil Nadu- 600004

Managed by

Jayprakash Somani Advocates & Solicitors

Law Firm for Supreme Court of India

Delhi Office

257 C, Pocket 1, Mayur Vihar Phase 1, Delhi 110091.

Call 8384051134, 9322188701, 8459194576, 9318381287 01141051516

Supreme Court Chamber

312, 3rd Floor, M. C. Setalvad Block, In front of 'D' Gate, Bhagwan Das Road, Supreme Court of India, New Delhi 110001

Contact: 8459194576, 9811011747,

www.jayprakashsomani.com

Books are available online at

1. Notion Press: https://notionpress.com/author/jayprakash_somani

2. Amazon: https://www.amazon.in/s?k=jayprakash+somani

3. Flipkart: https://www.flipkart.com/search?q=Jayprakash%20Somani

ONE

METERS AND INSTRUMENTS PRIVATE LIMITED AND ORS. VS. KANCHAN MEHTA, 2017

Hon'ble Judges/Coram: Adarsh Kumar Goel and U.U. Lalit, JJ.

Relevant Section:

Negotiable Instruments Act, 1881 - Section 138; Section 147; Code Of Criminal Procedure, 1973 (CrPC) - Section 258; Section 357(3)

Equivalent Citation: 2017(3)ACR2722, 2018(183)AIC193, AIR2017SC4594, 2017 (2) ALD(Crl.) 958 (SC), 2018 (102) ACC 953, 2017(6)ALT20, 2017 (3) ALT (Crl.) 317 (A.P.), IV(2017)BC315(SC), 2017(4)BLJ172, 2017(6)BomCR437, 2017(4)BomCR(Cri)392, I(2018)CCR47(SC), [2017]141CLA1(SC), (2018)1CompLJ13(SC), 2018CriLJ1160, 2017(4)Crimes1(SC), 2017(6)CTC66, 246(2018)DLT217, ILR2017(4)Kerala181, 2017(4)J.L.J.R.265, 2017(4)JCC267, 2017(6)JKJ82[SC], 2017 (5) KHC 177, 2017(4)KLT444, 2018-1-LW(Crl)464, 2018(4)MhLj1, 2018(3)MPLJ48, 2018(1)N.C.C.1, 2017(II)OLR1069, 2017(4)PLJR253, (2017)188PLR409, 2017(4)RCR(Criminal)476, 2017(4)RLW3376(SC), 2018(1)RLW202(SC), 2017(12)SCALE303, (2018)1SCC560, 2017 (9) SCJ 647, [2017]144SCL339(SC), 2017(3)UC2090, MANU/SC/0112/2017

No. of Pages in the Original Judgement: 8

Case Note:

Criminal - Compounding of offence - Exemption from appearance - Sections 138 and 147 of Negotiable Instruments Act, 1881 and Sections 258 and 357(3) of Code of Criminal Procedure, 1973 - Complaint was filed under Section 138 of Act - Magistrate after considering the complaint and the preliminary evidence, summoned Appellants - Magistrate in order observed that case could not be tried summarily as sentence of more than one year may have to be passed and be tried as summons case - Notice of accusation was served, 2nd Appellant, made statement that he was ready to make payment of cheque amount - Complainant declined to accept the demand draft - Case was adjourned for evidence - Appellants filed application under Section 147 of Act - Application was dismissed - High Court did not find any ground to interfere with order of Magistrate - Hence these appeals - Whether proceedings for offence under Section 138 of Act could be regulated where Accused was willing to deposit cheque amount.

Brief Facts of the case:

The Respondent filed complaint alleging that the Appellants were to pay a monthly amount to her under an agreement. Cheque was given in discharge of legal liability but the same was returned unpaid for want of sufficient funds. In spite of service of legal notice, the amount having not been paid, the Appellants committed the offence under Section 138 of the Act. The Magistrate vide order, after considering the complaint and the preliminary evidence, summoned the Appellants. The Magistrate in the order observed that the case could not be tried summarily as sentence of more than one year may have to be passed and be tried as summons case. Notice of accusation was served, 2nd Appellant, made a statement that he was ready to make the payment of the cheque amount. However, the complainant declined to accept the demand draft. The case was adjourned for evidence. The Appellants filed an application under Section 147 of the Act. The application was dismissed. The High Court did not find any ground to interfere with the order of the Magistrate. Hence these appeals.

In view of the above, we hold that where the cheque amount with interest and cost as assessed by the Court is paid by a specified date, the Court is entitled to close the proceedings in exercise of its powers Under Section 143 of the Act read with Section 258 Code of Criminal Procedure As already observed, normal Rule for trial of cases under Chapter XVII of the Act is to follow the summary procedure and summons trial procedure can be followed where sentence exceeding one year may be necessary taking into account the fact that compensation Under Section 357(3) Code of Criminal Procedure with sentence of less than one year will not be adequate, having regard to the amount of cheque, conduct of the Accused and other circumstances.

Held,

In every complaint Under Section 138 of the Act, it may be desirable that the complainant gives his bank account number and if possible e-mail ID of the Accused. If e-mail ID is available with the Bank where the Accused has an account, such Bank, on being required, should furnish such e-mail ID to the payee of the cheque. In every summons, issued to the Accused, it may be indicated that if the Accused deposits the specified amount, which should be assessed by the Court having regard to the cheque amount and interest/ cost, by a specified date, the Accused need not appear unless required and proceedings may be closed subject to any valid objection of the complainant. If the Accused complies with such summons and informs the Court and the complainant by e-mail, the Court can ascertain the objection, if any, of the complainant and close the proceedings unless it becomes necessary to proceed with the case. In such a situation, the Accused's presence can be required, unless the presence is otherwise exempted subject to such conditions as may be considered appropriate. The Accused, who wants to contest the case, must be required to disclose specific defence for such contest. It is open to the Court to ask specific questions to the Accused at that stage. In case the trial is to proceed, it will be open to the Court to explore the possibility of settlement. It will also be open to the Court to consider the provisions of plea bargaining. Subject to this, the trial can be on day to day basis and endeavour must be to conclude it within six months. The guilty must be punished at the earliest as per law and the one who obeys the law need not be held up in proceedings for long unnecessarily.

It will be open to the High Courts to consider and lay down category of cases where proceedings or part thereof can be conducted online by designated courts or otherwise. The High Courts may also consider issuing any further updated directions for dealing with Section 138 cases in the light of judgments of this Court.

The appeals are disposed of.

It will be open to the Appellants to move the Trial Court afresh for any further order in the light of this judgment.

TWO

NATIONAL SMALL INDUSTRIES CORP. LTD. VS. HARMEET SINGH PAINTAL AND ORS., 2017

Hon'ble Judges/Coram: P. Sathasivam and H.L. Dattu, JJ.

Relevant Section:

Negotiable Instruments Act, 1881 - Section 141

Equivalent Citation: 2010(2)ACR1221(SC), 2010(88)AIC227, 2010 (69) ACC 334, 2010ALLMR(Cri)921(SC), I(2010)BC674, I(2010)BC674(SC), 2010(2)BLJ39, 2010(2)BomCR565, I(2010)CCR344(SC), (2010)2CompLJ304(SC), (2010)2CompLJ304(SC), 2010CriLJ1907, 167(2010)DLT143(SC), (2010)51GLR1468, 2010GLH(2)766, JT2010(2)SC161, 2010 (2) KHC 355, 2010MPLJ86(SC), 2010(1)N.C.C.864, 2010(2)RCR(Criminal)122, 2010(2)SCALE372, (2010)3SCC330, [2010]98SCL407(SC), [2010]2SCR805, MANU/SC/1256/2017

No. of Pages in the Original Judgement: 7

Case Note:

Negotiable Instruments Act, 1881 - Sections 138 and 141-Dishonour of cheque-Offence by company-Vicarious liability of director-Scope of Section 141-On facts, held that respondent No. 1 was not vicariously liable-High Court justified in quashing summoning order-No merit in appeals.

Brief Facts of the case:

Leave granted in all the above special leave petitions.

The appeals arising out of S.L.P. (Criminal) Nos. 445- 461 of 2008 have been filed by the appellant-National Small Industries Corporation Limited against the common judgment and order dated 24.10.2007 passed by the High Court of Delhi at New Delhi in a batch of cases whereby the High Court quashed the summoning orders passed by the trial Court against respondent No. 1 - Harmeet Singh Paintal, under Section 138 read with Section 141 of the Negotiable Instruments Act, 1881 (for short "the Act")

Apart from the legal position with regard to compliance of Section 141 of the Act, in the appeals of National Small Industries Corporation, respondent No. 1- Harmeet Singh Paintal was no more a Director of the company when the cheques alleged in the complaint were signed and the same is evidenced from the Sixth Annual Report for the year 1996-97 of the accused company. The said report is of dated 30.08.1997 and the same was submitted with the Registrar of Companies on 05.12.1997 and assigned as document No. 42 dated 09.03.1998 by the Department. Those documents have been placed before this Court by respondent No. 1 as an additional document. In view of these particulars and in addition to the interpretation relating to Section 141 which we arrived at, no liability could be fastened on respondent No. 1. Further, it was pointed out that though he was an authorized signatory in the earlier transactions, after settlement and in respect of the present cause of action, admittedly fresh cheques were not signed by the first respondent. In the same way, in the appeal of the DCM Financial Services, the respondent therein, namely, Dev Sarin also filed additional documents to show that on the relevant date, namely the date of issuance of cheque he had no connection with the affairs of the company.

In the light of the above discussion and legal principles, we are in agreement with the conclusion arrived at by the High Court and in the absence of specific averment as to the role of the respondents and particularly in view of the acceptable materials that at the relevant time they were in no way connected with the affairs of the company, we reject all the contentions raised by learned Counsel for the appellants. Consequently, all the appeals fail and are accordingly dismissed.

THREE

A. CHITRA VS. N. BHUVANESHWARI, 2021

Hon'ble Judges/Coram: N.V. Ramana, Vineet Saran and V. Ramasubramanian, JJ.

Relevant Section:

Negotiable Instrument Act, 1881 - Section 138; Code of Criminal Procedure, 1973 (CrPC) - Section 357(3)

Equivalent Citation: 2021(2)RCR(Criminal)254, MANU/SC/1027/2021

No. of Pages in the Original Judgement: 2

Case notes:

criminal matters - matters challenging prosecution under negotiable instruments act

Brief Facts of the case:

The instant appeal, by way of special leave, is directed against order dated 18.03.2019 passed by the High Court of Judicature at Madras in Crl.R.C. No. 276 of 2019 whereby the High Court dismissed the Criminal Revision filed by the Appellant herein and upheld the conviction and sentence of 9 months simple imprisonment awarded to the Appellant Under Section 138 of the Negotiable Instruments Act with a direction to her to pay the compensation of ` 14,00,000/- (Rupees fourteen lakhs only) to the Respondent-complainant Under Section 357(3) of Code of Criminal Procedure, 1973 and in default to further undergo simple imprisonment for three months.

Held,

In view of the undertaking given by the learned Counsel for the Appellant as also the fact that the Appellant has already suffered incarceration for more than four months, we set aside the conviction and sentence awarded to the Appellant by the trial court as affirmed by the appellate Court and the High Court. The impugned order is accordingly set aside and the appeal is allowed.

The Registry is directed to release the amount of ` 7,00,000/- (Rupees seven lakhs only) deposited by the Appellant in the Registry of this Court along with interest, if any, accrued thereon, in favour of the Respondent-complainant after following the prescribed procedure.

Both the parties are directed to abide by the Deed of Memorandum of Understanding dated 18.10.2019 in its letter and spirit.

ppp

FOUR

GIMPEX PRIVATE LIMITED VS. MANOJ GOEL, 2021

Hon'ble Judges/Coram: Dr. D.Y. Chandrachud, Vikram Nath and B.V. Nagarathna, JJ.

Relevant Section:

Negotiable Instruments Act, 1881 - Section 138; Section 147; Code Of Criminal Procedure, 1973 (CrPC) - Section 258; Section 357(3)

Equivalent Citation: 2021(6)BLJ193, 2021 (3) MWN (Cr.) D.C.C. 81 MANU/SC/0829/2021

No. of Pages in the Original Judgement: 13

Case Note:

Criminal - Parallel prosecution - Quashing of Complaint - Cheque dishonour - Section 482 of the Code of Criminal Procedure, 1982 (CrPC) -Section 138 of the Negotiable Instruments Act 1881 (NI Act) - Compromise entered into between parties and new set of cheques replaced - New cheques also dishonoured followed by complaints - Whether parallel prosecutions arising from a single transactionsustainable?

Brief Facts of the case:

In the instant appeal, cheques in question were dishonoured upon presentation with an endorsement "payments stopped by drawer/ insufficient funds. A complaint was lodged by the Appellant under Sections 409 and 506(1) of the Indian Penal Code 1860, which was registered as an FIR. Appellant also got issued legal notices under Section 138 of the NI Actin respect of the dishonor of cheques. Complaints thereafter were filed. The parties thereafter entered into a deed of compromise to settle the matter. While the first complaint was pending, the cheques issued pursuant to the compromise deed were dishonoured leading to the second complaint under Section 138 of the NI Act. Both proceedings pending simultaneously. The issue arose for consideration was whether the complainant can be allowed to pursue both the cases or whether one of them must be quashed and the consequences resulting from such quashing.

For the above reasons, we hereby pass the following order:

Held,

(i) We are of the view that the Single Judge was in error in quashing the complaint CC No. 389/2017 pending on the file of the Seventh Metropolitan Magistrate, Chennai. The judgment of the Single Judge quashing the complaint is set aside;

(ii) Based on our analysis in Section C.1 above, we hereby quash the complaint CC Nos. 3326-3329 of 2012 and CC Nos. 99-101 of 2013.

56. As regards the companion appeal, we have already noted the submission of Mr. Jayant Bhushan that the issue as to whether the transaction was not a sale or otherwise could not have been enquired into in the course of the proceedings Under Section 482 Code of Criminal Procedure All the rights and contentions of the parties are kept open in the course of the trial. Accordingly Criminal Appeal No. 1068 of 2021 arising out of SLP (Criminal) No. 6564 of 2019 and Criminal Appeal Nos. 1069-1075 of 2021 arising out of SLP (Criminal) Nos. 7632-7638 of 2019 shall stand partially allowed in the above terms.

Pending application(s), if any, stand disposed of.

FIVE

TRIYAMBAK S. HEGDE VS. SRIPAD, 2021

Hon'ble Judges/Coram: N.V. Ramana, C.J.I., Surya Kant and A.S. Bopanna, JJ.

Relevant Section:

Code of Criminal Procedure, 1973 (CrPC) - Section 200; Section 313; Indian Penal Code, 1860 (IPC); Negotiable Instruments Act, 1881 - Section 118, Section 118(a), Section 138, Section 139

Equivalent Citation: 2021 (3) ALT (Crl.) 300 (A.P.), IV(2021)BC63(SC), 2021GLH(4)178, 2021GLH(4)178, 2021 (3) MWN (Cr.) D.C.C. 49, 2021(4)RCR(Criminal)250, MANU/SC/0690/2021

No. of Pages in the Original Judgement: 5

Case Note:

Criminal - Dishonour of cheque - Conviction - Section 138 of the Negotiable Instruments Act, 1881 - Transaction towards property sale - Respondent intending to sell not having title - Advance made demanded by Appellant - Cheque issued towards part repayment dishonoured - Complaint filed - Respondent convicted - High Court vide impugned judgment set aside conviction - Hence, the present appeal - Whether Respondent successfully rebutted the presumption so as to get acquitted?

Brief Facts of the case:

Appellant, as contended, was approached by Respondent and informed that due to his financial difficulty he intends to sell house. The Appellant agreed to purchase the same for the negotiated sale consideration. An agreement was executed and Respondent received advance amount. Subsequently, when the Appellant made certain enquiries, he learnt that the house stood in the name of father of the Respondent and the Respondent did not have the authority to sell the same. Appellant demanded the return of advance amount. The Respondent instead of paying the entire amount, issued a cheque being part of the amount, which got dishonoured with the endorsement 'insufficient funds'. Complaint for dishonour of cheque was filed and Respondent was convicted. Both preferred appeals. Appellant had sought enhancement of compensation directed. However, both the appeals were dismissed. High Court in further challenge allowed revision by Respondent and thereby conviction was set aside. Revision of Appellant was dismissed and hence the present appeal.

Having arrived at the above conclusion, it would be natural to restore the judgment of the Learned JMFC. Though in that regard, we confirm the order of conviction, we have given our thoughtful consideration relating to the appropriate sentence that is required to be imposed at this stage, inasmuch as; whether it is necessary to imprison the Respondent at this point in time or limit the sentence to imposition of fine. As noted, the transaction in question is not an out and out commercial transaction. The very case of the Appellant before the Trial Court was that the Respondent was in financial distress and it is in such event, he had offered to sell his house for which the advance payment was made by the Appellant. The subject cheque has been issued towards repayment of a portion of the advance amount since the sale transaction could not be taken forward. In that background, what cannot also be lost sight of is that more than two and half decades have passed from the date on which the transaction had taken place. During this period there would be a lot of social and economic change in the status of the parties. Further, as observed by this Court in Kaushalya Devi Massand v. RoopkishoreKhore MANU/SC/0385/2011 : (2011) 4 SCC 593, the gravity of complaint under N.I. Act cannot be equated with an offence under the provisions of the Indian Penal Code, 1860 or other criminal offences. In that view, in our opinion, in the facts and circumstances of the instant case, if an enhanced fine is imposed it would meet the ends of justice. Only in the event the Respondent-Accused not taking the benefit of the same to pay the fine but committing default instead, he would invite the penalty of imprisonment. Hence, appropriate modification is made to the sentence in the manner as indicated hereinbelow:

For all the aforestated reasons, the following order;

(i) The order dated 01.12.2009 passed by the High Court in Criminal Revision Petition No. 1282/2006 and 1481/2006 are set aside.

(ii) The conviction ordered in C.C. No. 790/2000 by the learned JMFC is restored.

(iii) The sentence to undergo simple imprisonment for six months and fine of Rs. 2,00,000/- (Rupees two lakhs only) is however modified. The Respondent/Accused is instead sentenced to pay the fine of Rs. 2,50,000/- (Rupees two lakhs fifty thousand only) within three months. In default of payment of fine the Respondent/Accused shall undergo simple imprisonment for six months.

(iv) From the fine amount, a sum of Rs. 2,40,000/- (Rupees two lakhs forty thousand only) shall be paid to the Appellant/Complainant as compensation.

(v) The Appeals No. 849-850/2011 are accordingly allowed in part.

(vi) The pending applications, if any, stand disposed of.

SIX

Ashutosh Ashok Parasrampuriya and Ors. Vs. Gharrkul Industries Pvt. Ltd. and Ors., 2021

Hon'ble Judges/Coram: Ajay Rastogi and Abhay Shreeniwas Oka, JJ.

Relevant Section:

Negotiable Instruments Act, 1881 - Section 138; Section 141

Equivalent Citation: AIR2021SC4898, AIR2021SC4898, 2021 (3) ALT (Crl.) 367 (A.P.), [2021]229CompCas1(SC), [2021]229CompCas1(SC), 2021 (3) MWN (Cr.) D.C.C. 72, MANU/SC/0838/2021

No. of Pages in the Original Judgement: 5

Case Note:

Criminal - Cheque dishonour - Complaint - Summoning - Quashing of complaint and order of summoning sought - Section 482 of Code of Criminal Procedure, 1973(CrPC) - Section 138 of Negotiable Instruments Act, 1881(NI Act) - Whether Appellants submits since complaint made no specific averment about they having committed offence and responsible for conduct of business of the Company cannot be made Accused in the proceedings - Whether in such circumstances Appellants merely being Directors can be made liable for prosecution?

Brief Facts of the case:

The Appellant Nos. 1 and 2 in Criminal Appeal @ SLP(Criminal) No. 7573 of 2014 and Appellant Nos. 2, 3 and 4 in Criminal Appeal @ SLP(Criminal) No. 9520 of 2014 are the Directors of the Appellant No. 1(Ameya Paper Mills Pvt. Ltd.) in Criminal Appeal @ SLP(Criminal) No. 9520 of 2014, the Private Limited Company established under the provisions of the Companies Act, 1956. It is the case of Respondent No. 1-complainant that it is a Private Limited Company dealing in the business of production and selling spices under the name and style of M/s. Gharkul Industries Private Ltd. and the Appellants being well acquainted with Respondent No. 1-complainant and being in need of financial assistance for their business approached Respondent No. 1-complainant with a request to provide them financial assistance. Respondent No. 1-complainant considering the relations and need of the Appellants provided financial assistance and on negotiations, Memorandum of Understanding was executed which was signed by Appellant No. 2-Dilip ShrikrishnaAndhare(Appellant No. 2 in Criminal Appeal @ SLP(Criminal) No. 9520 of 2014) with consent of all the Appellants in the presence of two attesting witnesses.

In our considered view, the High Court has rightly not interfered in exercise of its jurisdiction Under Section 482 Code of Criminal Procedure for quashing of the complaint.

Held,

Before concluding, we would like to observe that the proceedings could not be processed further in view of the interim order passed by this Court dated 17th October 2014 and because of the instant appeals, the other cases instituted by the Respondent(s)-complainant have been held up before the trial Court. Since these are the old cases instituted in the year 2012 and could not be processed further because of the pendency of the appeals in this Court, we may consider it appropriate to observe that let all the three cases of which a reference been made in para 17 of this judgment be clubbed together and be disposed of expeditiously as possible on its own merits in accordance with law without being influenced/inhibited by the observations made by us in the present judgment not later than six months from the date parties record their attendance before the trial Court. All the parties shall record their attendance before the concerned trial Court on 22nd November, 2021.

Consequently, the appeals fail and are accordingly dismissed.

Pending application(s), if any, stand disposed of.

SEVEN

ROHITBHAI JIVANLAL PATEL VS. STATE OF GUJARAT AND ORS., 2019

Hon'ble Judges/Coram: Abhay Manohar Sapre and Dinesh Maheshwari, JJ.

Relevant Section:

Negotiable Instruments Act, 1881 - Section 138

Equivalent Citation: 2019(201)AIC260, AIR2019SC1876, 2019 (2) ALD(Crl.) 385 (SC), 2019 (108) ACC 964, 2020 (2) ALT (Crl.) 458 (A.P.), II(2019)BC329(SC), [2019]150CLA494(SC), 2019CriLJ2400, 2019(1)Crimes291(SC), 2019(2)J.L.J.R.294, 2019(3)JCC1802, 2019(1)JKJ85[SC], 2019 (2) KHC 243, 2019(2)KLJ350, 2019(2)N.C.C.564, 2019(2)PLJR307, 2019(2)RCR(Criminal)559, 2019(5)SCALE138, (2019)18SCC106, 2019 (5) SCJ 140, [2019]153SCL273(SC), MANU/SC/0393/2019

No. of Pages in the Original Judgement: 10

Case Note:

Criminal - Conviction - Validity - Sections 118 and 139 and 138 of Negotiable Instrument Act, 1881 (NI Act) - Appeal was against impugned order of High Court disapproving acquittal of accused-Appellant while holding him guilty of offence under Section 138 of NI Act - Whether complainant-Respondent No. 2 had established ingredients of Sections 118 and 139 of NI Act, so as to justify drawing of presumption envisaged therein; and if so, as to whether accused-Appellant had been able to displace such presumption and to establish a probable defence whereby, onus would again shift to complainant.

Brief Facts of the case:

Accused-Appellant could not deny his signature on cheques in question that had been drawn in favour of complainant on a bank account maintained by Accused for a sum of Rs. 3 lakhs each. Said cheques were presented to Bank concerned within period of their validity and were returned unpaid for reason of either balance being insufficient or account being closed. All basic ingredients of Section 138 as also of Sections 118 and 139 were apparent on face of the record. Trial Court had also consciously taken note of these facts and had drawn requisite presumption. Therefore, it was required to be presumed that, cheques in question were drawn for consideration and holder of cheques i.e., complainant received same in discharge of an existing debt. Onus, therefore, shifts on accused-Appellant to establish a probable defence so as to rebut such a presumption.

In the singular and peculiar circumstances of this case, where the matters relating to 7 cheques issued by the Appellant in favour of Respondent No. 2 for a sum of Rs. 3 lakhs each are being considered together; and the Appellant is being penalised with double the amount of cheques in each case i.e., in all a sum of Rs. 42,00,000/-, in our view, the Appellant deserves to be extended another chance to mend himself by making payment of fine, of course, with the stipulation that in case of default in payment of the amount of fine, he would undergo simple imprisonment for a period of one year.

Held,

Therefore, this appeal is partly allowed in the following terms: The common judgment and order dated 08.01.2018 in R/Criminal Appeal No. 1187/2017 connected with R/Criminal Appeal Nos. 1191/2017 to 1196/2017 by the High Court of Gujarat at Ahmedabad is maintained as regards conviction of the accused-Appellant for the offence Under Section 138 of the Negotiable Instruments Act, 1881 for dishonour of 7 cheques in the sum of Rs. 3 lakhs each, as drawn by him in favour of the complainant-Respondent No. 2; however, the sentence is modified in the manner that in each of these 7 cases, the accused-Appellant shall pay fine to the extent of double the amount of each cheque (i.e., a sum of Rs. 6 lakhs in each case) within 2 months from today with the stipulation that in case of default in payment of fine, the accused-Appellant shall undergo simple imprisonment for a period of one year. On recovery of the amount of fine, the complainant-Respondent

No. 2 shall be compensated to the tune of Rs. 5.5 lakhs in each case. In the event of imprisonment for default in payment of fine, the sentences in all the 7 cases shall run concurrently.

The Trial Court shall take steps for enforcement of this judgment forthwith.

EIGHT

DASHRATH RUPSINGH RATHOD VS. STATE OF MAHARASHTRA, 2014

Hon'ble Judges/Coram: T.S. Thakur, Vikramajit Sen and C. Nagappan, JJ.

Relevant Section:

Negotiable Instruments Act, 1881 - Section 138

Equivalent Citation: 2014(3)ACR2914, 2014(7)ADJ115, 2014(141)AIC1, AIR2014SC3519, 2014 (2) ALD(Crl.) 190 (SC), 2014(5)ALD1(SC), 2014 (86) ACC 882, 2014ALLMR(Cri)3333(SC), 2014 (3) ALT (Crl.) 129 (SC), 2014(5)ALT33(SC), III(2014)BC513(SC), 2014(5)BomCR243, 2014(3)BomCR(Cri)593, 2014 (3) CCC 164 , III(2014)CCR428(SC), (SCSuppl)2014(4)CHN82, [2014]121CLA499(SC), [2015]191CompCas1(SC), (2014)3CompLJ414(SC), 2014CriLJ4350, 2014(3)Crimes162(SC), 2014(4)CTC666, 212(2014)DLT737(SC), 2014(145)DRJ1, 2014GLH(2)689, (2014)3GLR2700, 2015(2)GLT(SC)50, ILR2014(3)Kerala771, 2014(3)J.L.J.R.594, 2014(3)J.L.J.R.594, 2014 (3) JCC (NI) 147, 2014(4)JKJ14[SC], 2014(3) KarLJ 2313 (SC), 2014(5) KarLJ 499 (SC), 2014 (3) KHC 362 , 2014(3)KLJ600, 2014(3)KLT605(SC), 2015-1-LW(Crl)1, 2014(6)MhLj404, (2014) 3 MLJ(Crl) 475 (SC), 2014(4)MPHT257(SC), 2014(IV)MPJR(SC)1, 2014MPLJ407(SC), 2014(2)N.C.C.663, 2014(2)N.C.C.683, 2014(2)N.C.C.222, 2014(II)OLR587, 2014(II)OLR(SC)587, 2014(3)PLJR509, (2014)176PLR77, 2014(4)RCR(Civil), MANU/SC/0655/2014

No. of Pages in the Original Judgement: 16

Case Note:

Negotiable Instruments Act 1881

Brief Facts of the case:

The earliest and the most often quoted decision of this Court relevant to the present conundrum is **K. Bhaskaran** v. Sankaran Vaidhyan Balan MANU/SC/0625/1999 : (1999) 7 SCC 510 wherein a two-Judge Bench has, inter alia, interpreted Section 138 of the NI Act to indicate that, "the offence Under Section 138 can be completed only with the concatenation of a number of acts. Following are the acts which are components of the said offence: (1) Drawing of the cheque, (2) Presentation of the cheque to the bank, (3) Returning the cheque unpaid by the drawee bank, (4) Giving notice in writing to the drawer of the cheque demanding payment of the cheque amount, (5) Failure of the drawer to make payment within 15 days of the receipt of the notice." The provisions of Sections 177 to 179 of the Code of Criminal Procedure, 1973 (for short, 'Code of Criminal Procedure') have also been dealt with in detail. Furthermore, ***Bhaskaran*** in terms draws a distinction between 'giving of notice' and 'receiving of notice'. This is for the reason that Clause (b) of proviso to Section 138 of the NI Act postulates a demand being made by the payee or the holder in due course of the dishonoured cheque by giving a notice in writing to the drawer thereof. While doing so, the question of the receipt of the notice has also been cogitated upon.

Held,

An offence Under Section 138 of the Negotiable Instruments Act, 1881 is committed no sooner a cheque drawn by the accused on an account being maintained by him in a bank for discharge of debt/liability is returned unpaid for insufficiency of funds or for the reason that the amount exceeds the arrangement made with the bank.

(ii) Cognizance of any such offence is however forbidden Under Section 142 of the Act except upon a complaint in writing made by the payee or holder of the cheque in due course within a period of one month from the date the cause of action accrues to such payee or holder Under Clause (c) of proviso to Section 138.

(iii) The cause of action to file a complaint accrues to a complainant/payee/holder of a cheque in due course if

(a) the dishonoured cheque is presented to the drawee bank within a period of six months from the date of its issue.

(b) If the complainant has demanded payment of cheque amount within thirty days of receipt of information by him from the bank regarding the dishonour of the cheque and

(c) If the drawer has failed to pay the cheque amount within fifteen days of receipt of such notice.

(iv) The facts constituting cause of action do not constitute the ingredients of the offence Under Section 138 of the Act.

(v) The proviso to Section 138 simply postpones/defers institution of criminal proceedings and taking of cognizance by the Court till such time cause of action in terms of Clause (c) of proviso accrues to the complainant.

(vi) Once the cause of action accrues to the complainant, the jurisdiction of the Court to try the case will be determined by reference to the place where the cheque is dishonoured.

(vii) The general rule stipulated Under Section 177 of Code of Criminal Procedure applies to cases Under Section 138 of the Negotiable Instruments Act. Prosecution in such cases can, therefore, be launched against the drawer of the cheque only before the Court within whose jurisdiction the dishonour takes place except in situations where the offence of dishonour of the cheque punishable Under Section 138 is committed along with other offences in a single transaction within the meaning of Section 220(1) read with Section 184 of the Code of Criminal Procedure or is covered by the provisions of Section 182(1) read with Sections 184 and 220 thereof.

Before parting with this aspect of the matter, we need to remind ourselves that an avalanche of cases involving dishonour of cheques has come upon the Magistracy of this country. The number of such cases as of October 2008 were estimated to be more than 38 lakhs by the Law Commission of India in its 213th Report. The result is that cases involving dishonour of cheque is in all major cities choking the criminal justice system at the Magistrate's level. Courts in the four metropolitan cities and other commercially important centres are particularly burdened as the filing of such cases is in very large numbers. More than five lakh such cases were pending in criminal courts in Delhi alone as of 1st June 2008. The position is no different in other cities where large number of complaints are filed Under Section 138 not necessarily because the offence is committed in such cities but because multinational and other companies and commercial entities and agencies choose these places for filing the complaints for no better reason than the fact that notices demanding payment of cheque amounts were issued from such cities or the cheques were deposited for collection in their banks in those cities. Reliance is often placed on Bhaskaran's case to justify institution of such cases far away from where the transaction forming basis of the dishonoured cheque had taken place.

It is not uncommon to find complaints filed in different jurisdiction for cheques dishonoured in the same transaction and at the same place. This procedure is more often than not intended to use such oppressive litigation to achieve the collateral purpose of extracting money from the accused by denying him a fair opportunity to contest the claim by dragging him to a distant place. Bhaskaran's case could never have intended to give to the complainant/payee of the cheque such an advantage. Even so, experience has shown that the view taken in Bhaskaran's case permitting prosecution at any one of the five different places indicated therein has failed not only to meet the approval of other benches dealing with the question but also resulted in hardship, harassment and inconvenience to the accused persons. While anyone issuing a cheque is and ought to be made responsible if the same is dishonoured despite compliance with the provisions stipulated in the proviso, the Court ought to avoid an interpretation that can be used as an instrument of oppression by one of the parties. The unilateral acts of a complainant in presenting a cheque at a place of his choice or issuing a notice for payment of the dishonoured amount cannot in our view arm the complainant with the power to choose the place of trial. Suffice it to say, that not only on the Principles of Interpretation of Statutes but also the potential mischief which an erroneous interpretation can cause in terms of injustice and harassment to the accused the view taken in the Bhaskaran's case needs to be revisited as we have done in foregoing paragraphs.

NINE

A. NATARAJAN AND ORS. VS. T.R. RAJENDRAN, 2019

Hon'ble Judges/Coram: R. Banumathi and R. Subhash Reddy, JJ.

Equivalent Citation: 2019(2)RCR(Criminal)93, MANU/SC/0567/2019

Relevant Section:

Code of Criminal Procedure, 1973 (CrPC) - Section 320(8); Negotiable Instruments Act, 1981 - Section 138

No. of Pages in the Original Judgement: 1

Case Notes:

CRIMINAL MATTERS - MATTERS CHALLENGING PROSECUTION UNDER NEGOTIABLE INSTRUMENTS ACT

Brief Facts of the case:

Leave granted.

The Appellant-accused has been convicted Under Section 138 of the Negotiable Instruments Act, 1981 and was imposed a fine of ` 2,05,000/- (Rupees Two Lakhs Five Thousand) to be paid within a period of three months.Mr. Ragunath, learned Counsel appearing for the Appellants, and Mr. Mehul Gupta, learned Counsel appearing for the Respondent-complainant, submit that the Respondent-complainant has settled the matter with the Appellant-accused and to that effect they have filed a memorandum of understanding stating therein that they have amicably settled the matter.In view of the compromise deed entered into between the parties, the conviction of the Appellant is set aside in terms of Section 320(8) Code of Criminal Procedure and the Appellant is acquitted of all the charges.

Accordingly the appeal is allowed.

ÞÞÞ

TEN

S.M.S. Pharmaceuticals Ltd. Vs. Neeta Bhalla and Ors., 2005

Hon'ble Judges/Coram: Y.K. Sabharwal, Arun Kumar and B.N. Srikrishna, JJ.

Relevant Section:

NEGOTIABLE INSTRUMENTS ACT, 1881 - Section 138

Equivalent Citation: 2005(3)ACR3082(SC), 2005(34)AIC36, AIR2005SC3512, 2005(2)ALD(Cri)595, 2005 (53) ACC 503, 2005(5)ALLMR(SC)1118, IV(2005)BC425(SC), IV(2005)BC425(SC), 2006(1)BLJ244, 2005(3)BLJR2108, IV(2005)CCR12(SC), [2005]68CLA192(SC), [2005]127CompCas563(SC), (2005)6CompLJ144(SC), (2005)6CompLJ144(SC), 2005CriLJ4140, 2005(4)Crimes34(SC), 2005(5)CTC65, 123(2005)DLT275(SC), 2005(85)DRJ356, 2005GLH(3)513, JT2005(8)SC450, 2005(4)KLT209(SC), 2006-1-LW(Crl)1, 2005(4)MhLj731, 2005(4)MhLJ731(SC), 2006(1)MPJR(SC)97, 2005(4)PLJR148, (2006)142PLR689, 2005(4)RCR(Criminal)141, RLW2005(4)SC2386, 2005(7)SCALE397, (2005)8SCC89, [2005]63SCL93(SC), [2005]Supp(3)SCR371, [2005]148TAXMAN128(SC), MANU/SC/0622/2005

No. of Pages in the Original Judgement: 6

Case Note:

Negotiable Instruments Act, 1881

Brief Facts of the case:

This matter arises from a reference made by a two Judge Bench of this Court for determination of the following questions by a larger Bench :

Held,

"(a) whether for purposes of Section 141 of the Negotiable Instruments Act, 1881, it is sufficient if the substance of the allegation read as a whole fulfill the requirements of the said section and it is not necessary to specifically state in the complaint that the persons accused was in charge of, or responsible for, the conduct of the business of the company.

(b) whether a director of a company would be deemed to be in charge of, and responsible to, the company for conduct of the business of the company and, therefore, deemed to be guilty of the offence unless he proves to the contrary.

(c) even if it is held that specific averments are necessary, whether in the absence of such averments the signatory of the cheque and or the Managing Directors of Joint Managing Director who admittedly would be in charge of the company and responsible to the company for conduct of its business could be proceeded against."

In view of the above discussion, our answers to the questions posed in the Reference are as under:

(a) It is necessary to specifically aver in a complaint under Section 141 that at the time the offence was committed, the person accused was in charge of, and responsible for the conduct of business of the company. This averment is an essential requirement of Section 141 and has to be made in a complaint.

Without this averment being made in a complaint, the requirements of Section 141 cannot be said to be satisfied.

(b) The answer to question posed in sub-para (b) has to be in negative. Merely being a director of a company is not sufficient to make the person liable under Section 141 of the Act. A director in a company cannot be deemed to be in charge of and responsible to the company for conduct of its business. The requirement of Section 141 is that the person sought to be made liable should be in charge of and responsible for the conduct of the business of the company at the relevant time. This has to be averred as a fact as there is no deemed liability of a director in such cases.

(c) The answer to question (c) has to be in affirmative. The question notes that the Managing Director or Joint Managing Director would be admittedly in charge of the company and responsible to the company for conduct of its business. When that is so, holders of such positions in a company become liable under Section 141 of the Act. By virtue of the office they hold as Managing Director or Joint Managing Director, these persons are in charge of and responsible for the conduct of business of the company. Therefore, they get covered under Section 141. So far as signatory of a cheque which is dishonoured is concerned, he is clearly responsible for the incriminating act and will be covered under Sub-section (2) of Section 141.

The Reference having been answered, individual cases may be listed before appropriate Bench for disposal in accordance with law.

ELEVEN

In Re: Expeditious Trial of Cases Under Section 138 of N.I. Act 1881

Hon'ble Judges/Coram: S.A. Bobde, C.J.I., L. Nageswara Rao, B.R. Gavai, A.S. Bopanna and S. Ravindra Bhat, JJ.

Relevant Section:

Negotiable Instruments Act, 1881 - Section 138

Equivalent Citation: 2021(222)AIC111, AIR2021SC1957, 2021 (1) ALD(Crl.) 921 (SC), 2021 (116) ACC 609, 2021ALLMR(Cri)2641, 2021CriLJ2452, 2021GLH(2)381, ILR2021(2)Kerala555, 2021(2)J.L.J.R.181, 2021(3)JKJ154[SC], 2021(2)JLJ373, 2021(2)KCCR1793, 2021 (2) KHC 736, 2021(3)KLT10, 2021 (1) MWN (Cr.) D.C.C. 177, 2021(II)OLR121, 2021(2)PLJR321, 2021(2)RCR(Criminal)883, 2021(2)RLW1101(SC), [2021]167SCL103(SC),

No. of Pages in the Original Judgement: 6

Case Note:

Criminal - Dishonour of cheques - Section 138 of the Negotiable Instruments Act, 1881 (Act) - Dispute remained pending for past 16 years - Considering huge pendency of such cases instead case registered as Suo Motu - What guidelines/ methods could be resorted to ensure expeditioustrial of such cases?

Brief Facts of the case:

The present matter deals with the issue of large number of cases filed under Section 138 of the Negotiable Instruments Act, 1881 (Act) pending at various levels. The present was accordingly registered as Suo Motu Writ Petition (Criminal) captioned as "Expeditious Trial of Cases under Section 138 of N.I. Act 1881". The issue was raised considering gargantuan pendency of complaints having adverse effect in disposal of other criminal cases.

The upshot of the above discussion leads us to the following conclusions:

Held,

1) The High Courts are requested to issue practice directions to the Magistrates to record reasons before converting trial of complaints Under Section 138 of the Act from summary trial to summons trial.

2) Inquiry shall be conducted on receipt of complaints Under Section 138 of the Act to arrive at sufficient grounds to proceed against the Accused, when such Accused resides beyond the territorial jurisdiction of the court.

3) For the conduct of inquiry Under Section 202 of the Code, evidence of witnesses on behalf of the complainant shall be permitted to be taken on affidavit. In suitable cases, the Magistrate can restrict the inquiry to examination of documents without insisting for examination of witnesses.

4) We recommend that suitable amendments be made to the Act for provision of one trial against a person for multiple offences Under Section 138 of the Act committed within a period of 12 months, notwithstanding the restriction in Section 219 of the Code.

5) The High Courts are requested to issue practice directions to the Trial Courts to treat service of summons in one complaint Under Section 138 forming part of a transaction, as deemed service in respect of all the complaints filed before the same court relating to dishonour of cheques issued as part of the said transaction.

6) Judgments of this Court in Adalat Prasad (supra) and Subramanium Sethuraman (supra) have interpreted the law correctly and we reiterate that there is no inherent power of Trial Courts to review or recall the issue of summons. This does not affect the power of the Trial Court Under Section 322 of the Code to revisit the order of issue of process in case it is brought to the court's notice that it lacks jurisdiction to try the complaint.

7) Section 258 of the Code is not applicable to complaints Under Section 138 of the Act and findings to the contrary in Meters and Instruments (supra) do not lay down correct law. To conclusively deal with this aspect, amendment to the Act empowering the Trial Courts to reconsider/recall

summons in respect of complaints Under Section 138 shall be considered by the Committee constituted by an order of this Court dated 10.03.2021.

8) All other points, which have been raised by the Amici Curiae in their preliminary report and written submissions and not considered herein, shall be the subject matter of deliberation by the aforementioned Committee. Any other issue relating to expeditious disposal of complaints Under Section 138 of the Act shall also be considered by the Committee.

List the matter after eight weeks. Further hearing in this matter will be before 3-Judges Bench.

We place on record our appreciation for the valuable assistance rendered by Mr. Sidharth Luthra, learned Senior Counsel and Mr. K. Parameshwar, learned Counsel, as Amici Curiae.

TWELVE

KALAMANI TEX AND ORS. VS. P. BALASUBRAMANIAN, 2021

Hon'ble Judges/Coram:N.V. Ramana, Surya Kant and Aniruddha Bose, JJ.

Relevant Sections:

Negotiable Instruments Act, 1881 - Section 118, Section 138, Section 139, Section 142

Equivalent Citation: 2021(3)ACR2672, 2021(219)AIC184, 2021 (115) ACC 322, 2021ALLMR(Cri)1594, 2021 (2) ALT (Crl.) 178 (A.P.), III(2021)BC209(SC), 2021(2)BLJ226, 2021(1)Crimes202(SC), 2021(2)CTC357, 2021(1)ICC1001, ILR2021(1)Kerala855, 2021(1)JKJ63[SC], 2021(1)KCCR545, 2021 (2) KHC 517, 2021(5)MhLj632, 2021(4)MPLJ38, 2021 (1) MWN (Cr.) D.C.C. 49, 2021(1)N.C.C.763, (2021)202PLR746, 2021(2)RCR(Criminal)160, (2021)5SCC283, 2021 (1) SCJ 720, [2021]165SCL538(SC), 2021(2)UC647MANU/SC/0066/2021

No. of Pages in the Original Judgement: 8

Case Note:

Criminal - Conviction - Dishonour of cheque - Sections 118, 138, 139 and 142 of Negotiable Instruments Act, 1881 - Respondent along with Appellant No. 1 was engaged in business arrangement, whereby they agreed to jointly export garments - Certain issues arose regarding delays in shipment and payment from buyer, due to which, Appellants had to pay Respondent sum - Appellant No. 2 issued cheque on behalf of Appellant No. 1 in favour of

Respondent and also executed Deed of Undertaking undertook to pay Respondent - Respondent presented said cheque to bank which was disnohoured - Respondent then lodged private complaint under Section 138 and 142 of Act before Judicial Magistrate - Trial Court disbelieved observed that Respondent had failed to establish legally enforceable liability on date of issue of cheque, thus complaint was liable to be dismissed - Respondent preferred criminal appeal before High Court - High Court allowed criminal appeal and convicted both Appellants under Section 138 of Act - Hence, present appeal - Whether High Court erred in reversing judgment of acquittal into conviction for offence punishable under Section 138 of Act.

Brief Facts of the case:

The Respondent along with Appellant No. 1 was engaged in a business arrangement, whereby they agreed to jointly export garments. Certain issues arose regarding delays in shipment and payment from the buyer, due to which, the Appellants had to pay the Respondent a sum. To that end, Appellant No. 2 issued a cheque on behalf of Appellant No. 1 in favour of the Respondent and also executed a Deed of Undertaking on the same day wherein Appellant No. 2 personally undertook to pay the Respondent in lieu of the initial expenditure incurred by the latter. The Respondent presented the said cheque to the bank for collection but it was returned with an endorsement that there were insufficient funds in the account of Appellants. In wake of the cheque being dishonoured, the Respondent issued a notice asking the Appellants to pay the amount within fifteen days. The Respondent then lodged a private complaint Under Section 138 and 142 of the NIA read with Section 200 of the Code of Criminal Procedure, 1973 before the Judicial Magistrate. The trial Court disbelieved the Respondent's claim and observed that he had failed to establish a legally enforceable liability on the date of issue of cheque. The Court held that since the basic ingredients of an offence under Section 138 of the NIA were not satisfied, the complaint was liable to be dismissed. Discontented with the order of the trial Court, the Respondent preferred a criminal appeal before the High Court, wherein, the Court noted that Appellant No. 2 had admitted his signatures on both the Cheque and the Deed of Undertaking and had thus acknowledged the Appellants' liability. The High Court therefore vide impugned judgment allowed the criminal appeal and convicted both the Appellants under Section 138 of NIA.

Held,

(i) Once the second Appellant had admitted his signatures on the cheque and the Deed, the trial Court ought to have presumed that the cheque was issued as consideration for a legally enforceable debt. The trial Court fell in error when it called upon the Complainant-Respondent to explain the circumstances under which the Appellants were liable to pay. Such approach of the trial Court was directly in the teeth of the established legal position, and amounts to a patent error of law.

(ii) The Appellants had banked upon the evidence of Assistant Manager of bank to dispute the existence of any recoverable debt. However, his deposition merely highlights that the Respondent had an over-extended credit facility with the bank and his failure to update his account led to debt recovery proceedings. Such evidence did not disprove the Appellants' liability and had a little bearing on the merits of the Respondent's complaint. Similarly, the Appellants' mere bald denial regarding genuineness of the Deed of Undertaking, despite admitting the signatures of Appellant No. 2 thereupon, did not cast any doubt on the genuineness of the said document.

(iii) Considering the fact that there had been an admitted business relationship between the parties, the defence raised by the Appellants did not inspire confidence or meet the standard of preponderance of probability. In the absence of any other relevant material, it appears that the High Court did not erred in discarding the Appellants' defence and upholding the onus imposed upon them in terms of Section 118 and Section 139 of the NIA.

THIRTEEN

JIK Industries Limited and Ors. Vs. Amarlal V. Jumani and Ors., 2012

Hon'ble Judges/Coram: A.K. Ganguly and J.S. Khehar, JJ.

Relevant Section:

Negotiable Instruments Act, 1881 - Section 138; Negotiable Instruments Act, 1881 - Section 141

Equivalent Citation: 2012(111)AIC41, AIR2012SC1079, 2012(2)ALD(Cri)441, 2013(1)ALT(Cri)SC240, I(2012)BC646, 2012(3)B.L.J.292, 2012BomCR(Cri)593, I(2012)CCR329(SC), [2012]107CLA192(SC), (2012)2CompLJ46(SC), 2012CriLJ1649, 2012(1)Crimes204(SC), 2012(3)CTC428, [2012(2)JCR277(SC)], JT2012(2)SC1, 2012-1-LW(Crl)637, 2012(4)MhLj568, 2012MLJ(Crl)703, 2012(1)N.C.C.509, 2012(1)RCR(Civil)913, 2012(1)RCR(Criminal)822, 2012(2)SCALE97, (2012)3SCC255, [2012]112SCL51(SC), 2012(1)UC449 , MANU/SC/0075/2012

No. of Pages in the Original Judgement: 6

Case Note:

Criminal - Compounding of Offences - Sections 138, 141 of Negotiable Instruments Act, 1881 (N.I. Act); Sections 4 (2), 320 of Criminal Procedure Code, 1973 (CrPC); Section 391 of Companies Act, 1956 - High Court dismissed several criminal writ Petitions which were filed challenging processes which were issued by Trial Judge on complaint filed by Respondents in proceedings under Section 138 read with Section 141 of N.I. Act - Held, effect of approval of a scheme of compromise and arrangement under Section 391 of Act was that, it bound dissenting minority, company as also liquidator if company was under winding up - Therefore, Section 391 of Act, gave very wide discretion to Court to approve any set of arrangement between company and its shareholders - A scheme under Section 391 of Act, did not have effect of creating new debt - Scheme simply made original debt payable in a manner and to extent provided for in scheme - In instant appeal, in most of cases offence under N.I. Act had been committed prior to scheme - Therefore, offence which had already been committed prior to scheme did not get automatically compounded only as a result of said scheme - Therefore, it could not be said that, scheme under Section 391 of Act, would have effect of automatically compounding offence under N.I. Act - A scheme under Section 391 of Act, was binding on all shareholders including those who oppose it from being sanctioned - Jurisdiction of Company Court while sanctioning scheme was supervisory - A scheme under Section 391 of Act could not be unfair or contrary to public policy, nor could it be unconscionable or against law - A scheme under Section 391 of Act could not have effect of overriding requirement of any law - Compounding of an offence was always controlled by statutory provision - There were various features in compounding of an offence and those features must be satisfied before it could be claimed by offender that offence had been compounded - Thus, compounding of an offence could not be achieved indirectly by sanctioning of a scheme by Company Court - Quashing of a case was different from compounding - In quashing Court applied it but in compounding it was primarily based on consent of injured party - Therefore, two could not be equated - Compounding of an offence was statutorily provided under Section 320 of CrPC - There were basically two categories of offences under provisions of Indian Penal Code which had been made compoundable - Representation of person compounding had been statutorily provided in all situations - Under Scheme of modern legislation, non-obstante clause had a contextual and limited application - In instant case, non-obstante clause used in Section 147 of N.I. Act did not refer to any particular section of Code of Criminal Procedure but referred to entire Code - When non-obstante clause was used in aforesaid fashion then extent of its impact had to be found out on basis of consideration of intent and purpose of insertion of such a clause - Offence under N.I. Act, which was previously non-compoundable in view of Section 320 (9) of CrPC had now become compoundable - That did not mean that effect of Section 147 was to obliterate all statutory provisions of Section 320 of CrPC relating to mode and manner of compounding of an offence - Section 147 would only override Section 320 (9) of CrPC in so far as offence under Section 147 of N.I. Act was concerned - In instant case no special procedure had been prescribed under N.I. Act relating to compounding of an offence - In absence of special procedure relating to compounding, procedure relating to compounding under Section 320 would automatically apply in view of clear mandate of Section 4 (2) of CrPC - In view of Section 4 (2) of CrPC, basic procedure of compounding an offence laid down in Section 320 of CrPC would apply to compounding of an offence under N.I. Act - A judgment was always an authority for what it decided - A judgment could not be read as a statute - It had to be read in context of facts discussed in it - Basic mode and manner of effecting compounding of an offence under Section 320 of CrPC could not be said to be not attracted in case of compounding of an offence under N.I. Act in view of Section 147 of same - Compounding was permitted in certain categories of cases where rights of public in general were not affected but in all cases such compounding was permissible with consent of injured party - Provisions contained in Section 320 of CrPC and various Sub-sections was a Code by itself relating to compounding of offence - It provided for various parameters and procedures and guidelines in matter of compounding - There was no other statutory procedure for compounding of offence under N.I. Act - Therefore, Section 147 of N.I. Act must be reasonably construed to mean that as a result of said Section offences under N.I. Act were made compoundable, but main principle of such compounding, namely, consent of person aggrieved or person injured or complainant could not be wished away nor could same be substituted by virtue of Section 147 of N.I. Act - It could not be said that as a result of sanction of a scheme under Section 391 of Act there was an automatic compounding of offences under Section 138 of N.I. Act even without consent of Complainant - Judgment of High Court was affirmed

Brief facts of the case:

This group of appeals were heard together as they involve common questions of law. There are some factual differences but the main argument by the Appellant(s) in this matter was advanced by Mr. Chander Uday Singh, Senior Advocate on behalf of the Sharp Industries Limited in SLP (Crl.) No. 6643-6651 of 2010 and the facts are taken mostly from the said case.

3. The Learned Counsel assailed the judgment of the High Court wherein by a detailed judgment High Court dismissed several criminal writ petitions which were filed challenging the processes which were issued by the learned Trial Judge on the complaint filed by the Respondents in proceedings under Section 138 read with Section 141 of Negotiable Instruments Act, 1881 (hereinafter 'N.I. Act'). By way of a detailed judgment, the High Court after dismissing the writ petitions held that sanction of a scheme under Section 391 of the Companies Act, 1956 (hereinafter 'Companies Act') does not amount to compounding of an offence under Section 138 read with Section 141 of the N.I. Act. The High Court also held that sanction of a scheme under Section 391 of the Companies Act will not have the effect of termination or dismissal of complaint proceedings under Negotiable Instruments Act. However, the learned Judge made it clear that the judgment of the High Court will not prevent the Petitioners from filing separate application invoking the provisions of Section 482 Code of Criminal Procedure, if they are so advised. Assailing the said judgment the Learned Counsel submitted that an unsecured creditor who does not oppose the scheme of compromise or arrangement under Section 391 of the Companies Act must be taken to have supported the scheme in its entirety once such a scheme is sanctioned by the High Court, even a dissenting creditor cannot file a criminal complaint under Section 138 of the N.I. Act for enforcement of a pre-compromise debt. Nor can such a creditor oppose the compounding of criminal complaint which was filed under Section 138 of the Negotiable Instruments Act in respect of pre-compromise debt.

Held,

In our country also when the Criminal Procedure Code, 1861 was enacted it was silent about the compounding of offence. Subsequently, when the next Code of 1872 was introduced it mentioned about compounding in Section 188 by providing the mode of compounding. However, it did not contain any provision declaring what offences were compoundable. The decision as to what offences were compoundable was governed by reference to the exception to Section 214 of the Indian Penal Code. The subsequent Code of 1898 provided Section 345 indicating the offences which were compoundable but the said Section was only made applicable to compounding of offences defined and permissible under Indian Penal code. The present Code, which repealed the 1898 Code, contains Section 320 containing comprehensive provisions for compounding.

A perusal of Section 320 makes it clear that the provisions contained in Section 320 and the various Sub-sections is a Code by itself relating to compounding of offence. It provides for the various parameters and procedures and guidelines in the matter of compounding. If this Court upholds the contention of the Appellant that as a result of incorporation of Section 147 in the Negotiable Instruments Act, the entire gamut of procedure of Section 320 of the Code are made inapplicable to compounding of an offence under the N.I. Act, in that case the compounding of offence under Negotiable Instruments Act will be left totally unguided or uncontrolled. Such an interpretation apart from being an absurd or unreasonable one will also be contrary to the provisions of Section 4(2) of the Code, which has been discussed above. There is no other statutory procedure for compounding of offence under N.I. Act. Therefore, Section 147 of the Negotiable Instruments Act must be reasonably construed to mean that as a result of the said Section the offences under N.I. Act are made compoundable, but the main principle of such compounding, namely, the consent of the person aggrieved or the person injured or the complainant cannot be wished away nor can the same be substituted by virtue of Section 147 of N.I. Act.

For the reasons aforesaid, this Court is unable to accept the contentions of the Learned Counsel for the Appellant(s) that as a result of sanction of a scheme under Section 391 of the Companies Act there is an automatic compounding of offences under Section 138 of the Negotiable Instruments Act even without the consent of the complainant.

The appeals are dismissed. The judgment of the High Court is affirmed.

FOURTEEN

VEERA EXPORTS VS. T. KALAVATHY, 2001

Hon'ble Judges/Coram: K.T. Thomas and S.N. Variava, JJ.

Relevant Section:NEGOTIABLE INSTRUMENTS ACT, 1881 - Section 87

Equivalent Citation: 2002(1)ACR86(SC), AIR2002SC38, 2001(2)ALD(Cri)915, 2002 (44) ACC 306, 2002(1)ALLMR(SC)275, 2002 (46) ALR 43, 2002(1)ALT(Cri)41, 2002 (1) AWC 28 (SC), I(2002)BC278(SC), I(2002)BC278(SC), IV(2001)CCR270(SC), (SCSuppl)2002(1)CHN1, [2001]107CompCas594(SC), (2002)1CompLJ52(SC), (2002)1CompLJ52(SC), (2002)1CompLJ52(SC), 2002CriLJ203, 2002(1)Crimes123(SC), JT2001(9)SC368, 2001(2)KLJ997, 2002(1)KLT58(SC), 2002-1-LW(Crl)361, 2002(1)PLJR158, 2002(1)RCR(Criminal)682, RLW2002(1)SC69, 2001(7)SCALE609, (2002)1SCC97, [2002]38SCL665(SC)MANU/SC/0699/2001

No. of Pages in the Original Judgement: 5

Case Note:

Negotiable Instruments Act, 1881 - Section 138 -- A cheque which has become invalid because of the expiry of the stipulated period could be made valid by alteration of dates -- It is always open to a drawer to voluntarily revalidate a negotiable instrument, including a cheque.

Brief facts of the case:

The Respondent had issued to the Appellants 8 cheques, bearing various dates from 9th April, 1995 to 30th April, 1995, for a sum totalling Rs. 4 lacs. The cheques were presented for payment on 15th May, 1995 but were dishonoured. It is the case of the Appellant that the fact of dishonour was brought to the notice of the Respondent and that the Respondent then requested for more time to pay. The Appellants claim that they granted her, more time to pay. The Appellants claim that as the Respondent still could not pay the amounts, in January, 1996, she changed the date of the cheques from 1995 to 1996. The Appellants claim that the Respondent also made the necessary endorsement on the cheques at that time. The Appellant claim that the Respondent then requested the Appellant to present the cheques after a period of three months.

The cheques were again presented on 18th July, 1996 and were dishonoured. A legal notice dated 8th August, 1996 was served upon the Respondent. The Respondent, by her reply dated 23rd August, 1996, alleged that she had been forced to change the dates against her will. She also took up some other contentions. The Appellant then filed a complaint under Section 138 of the Negotiable Instruments Act.

The Respondent thereafter filed a petition in the High Court of Madras to quash the complaint. By the impugned order dated 24th November, 2000, the High Court has quashed the complaint.

Held,

There is no provision in the Negotiable Instruments Act or in any other law which stipulates that a drawer of a negotiable instrument cannot revalidate it. It is always open to a drawer to voluntarily revalidate a negotiable instrument, including a cheque. The provisions of this section are subject to those of Sections 20, 49, 86 and 125". The first paragraph of Section 87 makes it clear that the party who consents to the alteration as well as the party who made the alteration are disentitled to complain against such alteration, e.g. if the drawer of the cheque himself altered the cheque for validating or revalidating the same instrument he cannot take advantage of it later by saying that the cheque became void as there is material alteration thereto. Further, even if the payee or the holder of the cheque made the alteration with the consent of the drawer thereof, such alteration also cannot be used as a ground to resist the right of the payee or the holder thereof. It is always a question of fact whether the alteration was made by the drawer himself or whether it was made with the consent of the drawer. It requires evidence to prove the aforesaid question whenever it is disputed. There is no provision in the Negotiable Instruments Act or in any other law which stipulates that a drawer of a negotiable instrument cannot re-validate it. It is always open to a drawer to voluntarily revalidate a negotiable instrument, including a cheque.

FIFTEEN

Ashok Yeshwant Badavevs. Surendra Madhavrao Nighojakar and Ors., 2001

Hon'ble Judges/Coram: K.T. Thomas, R.P. Sethi and B.N. Agrawal, JJ.

Relevant Section:

Negotiable Instruments Act, 1881 - Section 138

Equivalent Citation: 2001(2)ACR1083(SC), AIR2001SC1315, 2001(1)ALD(Cri)668, 2001 (42) ACC 788, 2001ALLMR(Cri)1028(SC), 2001(2)ALT(Cri)11, II(2001)BC1(SC), 2001(103(2))BOMLR913, I(2001)CCR358(SC), (2001)2CompLJ270(SC), 2001CriLJ1674, JT2001(3)SC508, 2001(2)KLT28(SC), 2001(2)PLJR122, 2001(2)RCR(Criminal)165, 2001(2)SCALE472, (2001)3SCC726, [2001]2SCR426, 2001(1)UC538, 2001(1)UC632, 2001(2)UJ1024, MANU/SC/0170/2001

No. of Pages in the Original Judgement: 5

Case Note:

Negotiable Instruments Act, 1881-- Sections 5, 6, 19, 138, 139 and 140-- Dishonour of cheque--:Post dated cheque--Six months period shall be reckoned from date mentioned on face of cheque.

Brief facts of the case:

Challenge in this appeal has been made to judgment passed by the Bombay High Court dismissing writ application filed by the appellant upholding an order passed by a Sessions Court in revision refusing to interfere with the order passed by a Chief Judicial Magistrate taking cognizance and issuing process against the appellant for the offence under Section 138 of the Negotiable Instruments Act, 1881 (hereinafter referred to as 'the Act').

3. Surendra Madhavrao Nighojkar - respondent No. 1 filed a petition of complaint in the Court of Chief Judicial Magistrate, Satara on 2.9.1996 for prosecution of the appellant under Section 138 of the Act besides Section 420 of the Penal Code which was registered as Criminal Case No. 11348/ 96. Case of the complainant in, short, is that on 4.7.1993 an agreement to sell was executed by the complainant for sale of his 1/3rd share in CTS No. 189 within Pratapganj Peth in the district of Satara for Rs. 2,21,000/- and the said sale was required to be executed in the name of mother and wife of the appellant. At the time of agreement, Rs. 50,000/- was paid by the accused to the complainant. Thereafter on 10.11.1995 sale deed was scribed and on that date a further sum of Rs. 1,25,000/- was paid by the accused to the complainant besides a post-dated cheque drawn on State Bank of India, Satara Branch, for Rs. 46,000/- bearing the date as 20.1.1996 which was made over by the accused to the complainant. Later on, the accused on several occasions made a request to the complainant for not presenting the cheque in the bank as he was not having sufficient funds in his bank account which request was acceded to by the complainant. Ultimately, as the period of six months was going to expire on 19.7.1996, the complainant had no option but to present the said cheque before his banker for encashment, but the same was returned without clearance on 11-7-1996 with the endorsement "account closed". From these facts complainant deduced that the accused had deceived him which necessitated issuance of notice by the complainant to the accused on 22.7.1996 which was refused by him on 6.8.1996 whereafter the present complaint was filed.

Held,

As the payment was conditional it would only be good when the cheque is presented on the date it bears, namely, February 25, 1954 and is honoured. The earliest date, therefore, on which the respondent could have realised the cheque which he had received as conditional payment on February 4, 1954 was the 25th February, 1954 if he had presented it on that date and it had been honoured."

From a bare perusal of Sections 5 & 6 of the Act it would appear that bill of exchange is a negotiable instrument in writing containing an instruction to a third party to pay a stated sum of money at a designated future date or on demand. On the other hand, a 'cheque' is a bill of exchange drawn on a bank by the holder of an account payable on demand. Under Section 6 of the Act a 'cheque' is also a bill of exchange but it is drawn on a banker and payable on demand. A bill of exchange even though drawn on a banker, if it is not payable on demand, it is not a cheque. A 'post-dated cheque' is not payable till the date which is shown thereon arrives and will become cheque on the said date and prior to that date the same remains bill of exchange.

For prosecuting a person for an offence under Section 138 of the Act, it is inevitable that the cheque is presented to the banker within a period of six months from the date on which it is drawn or within the period of its validity whichever is earlier. When a post dated cheque is written or drawn, it is only a bill of exchange and so long the same remains a bill of exchange, the provisions of Section 138 are not applicable to the said instrument. The post-dated cheque becomes a cheque within the meaning of Section 138 of the Act on the date which is written thereon and the 6 months period has to be reckoned for the purposes of proviso (a) to Section 138 of the Act from the said date. Thus while respectfully agreeing with the law laid down by this Court in the case of Anil Kumar Sawhney, we hold that six months period shall be reckoned from the date mentioned on the face of the cheque and not any earlier date on which the cheque was made over by the drawer to the drawee.

In the case on hand, the cheque was prepared and made over by the drawer to the drawee on 10.11.1995 but the date mentioned thereon was 20.1.1996 and it was presented before the banker for encashment on 7.7.1996, i.e., within a period of six months from 20.1.1996. Thus we find no ground to quash prosecution of the appellant as, on the facts alleged, an offence under Section 138 of the Act is clearly made out.

The appeal is accordingly dismissed.

SIXTEEN

Mandvi Co-op. Bank Ltd. Vs. Nimesh B. Thakore, 2010

Hon'ble Judges/Coram: Tarun Chatterjee and Aftab Alam, JJ.

Relevant Section:

Negotiable Instruments Act, 1881 - Section 138; Code of Criminal Procedure, 1973 (CrPC) - Section 296; Indian Penal Code, 1860 (IPC) - Section 498A

Equivalent Citation: 2010(1)ACR522(SC), 2010(86)AIC178, AIR2010SC1402, 2010 (68) ACC 670, 2010ALLMR(Cri)599(SC), I(2010)BC600, I(2010)BC600(SC), 2010(1)BomCR614, 2010 (1) CCC 182 , I(2010)CCR215(SC), [2010]98CLA178(SC), CLT(2010)Supp.Crl.462, 2010(1)CTC693, I(2010)DLT150(SC), (2010)2GLR990, JT2010(1)SC259, 2010(1)KLT321(SC), 2010(2)MPHT397, 2010MPLJ42(SC), 2010(I)OLR(SC)306, 2010(1)RCR(Criminal)68, 2010(1)RCR(Criminal)681, RLW2010(3)SC2554, 2010(1)SCALE188, (2010)3SCC83, [2010]98SCL139(SC), [2010]1SCR219, 2010(1)UC223, 2010(1)UJ454, MANU/SC/0016/2010

No. of Pages in the Original Judgement: 10

Case Note:

(1) Negotiable Instruments Act, 1881 - Section 145 (2)-Summoning person/ complainant giving evidence on affidavit-Whether accused can insist that person so summoned should first give deposition in examination-in-chief before being cross-examined by him?-Held, "no".

What Section 145 (2) of the Negotiable Instruments Act, 1881 (Act) says is simply this. The Court may, at its discretion, call a person giving his evidence on affidavit and examine him as to the facts contained therein. But if an application is made either by the prosecution or by the accused the Court must call the person giving his evidence on affidavit, again to be examined as to the facts contained therein. What would be the extent and nature of examination in each case is a different matter and that has to be reasonably construed in light of the provision of Section 145 (1) and having regard to the object and purpose of the entire scheme of Sections 143 to 146. The scheme of Sections 143 to 146 does not in any way affect the Judge's powers under Section 165 of the Evidence Act. As a matter of fact, Section 145 (2) expressly provides that the Court may, if it thinks fit, summon and examine any person giving evidence on affidavit. But how would the person giving evidence on affidavit be examined, on being summoned to appear before the Court on the application made by the prosecution or the accused? The affidavit of the person so summoned that is already on the record is obviously in the nature of examination-in-chief. Hence, on being summoned on the application made by the accused the deponent of the affidavit (the complainant or any of his witnesses) can only be subjected to cross-examination as to the facts stated in the affidavit. In so far as the prosecution is concerned the occasion to summon any of its witnesses who has given his evidence on affidavit may arise in two ways. The prosecution may summon a person who has given his evidence on affidavit and has been cross-examined for "reexamination". The prosecution may also have to summon a witness whose evidence is given on affidavit in case objection is raised by the defence regarding the validity and/or sufficiency of proof of some document(s) submitted alongwith the affidavit. In that event the witness may be summoned to appear before the Court to cure the defect and to have the document(s) properly proved by following the correct legal mode. This appears to us as the simple answer to the above question and the correct legal position. Any other meaning given to sub-section (2) of Section 145, would make the provision of Section 145 (1) nugatory and would completely defeat the very scheme of trial as designed under Sections 143 to 147.

Hence, notwithstanding the apparent verbal similarity between Section 145 (2) of the Act and Section 296 (2), Cr. P.C., it would be completely wrong to interpret the true scope and meaning of the one in the light of the other. Neither the legislative history of Section 296 (2) nor any decision on that section can persuade us to hold that under Section 145 (2) of the Act, on being summoned at the instance of the accused the complainant or any of his witnesses should be first made to depose in examination-in-chief before cross-examination.

(2) Negotiable Instruments Act, 1881 - Section 145 (1) and (2)-Whether provisions of sub-sections (1) and (2) of Section 145 would apply to proceedings pending on February 6, 2003 date on which those provisions inserted in Act?-Held, "yes"-Those provisions are not substantive but only procedural in nature-And would undoubtedly apply to pending cases.

(3) Negotiable Instruments Act, 1881 - Section 145 (1)-Right to give evidence on affidavit-Whether this right provided to complainant under Section 145 (1) also available to accused?-Held, "no"-High Court erroneously held otherwise-High Court's direction in that behalf set aside.

Brief Facts of the case:

In these appeals we are required to consider the special provisions laid down by Section 145 of the Negotiable Instruments Act, 1881 (`the Act', hereinafter) for a dishonoured cheque trial and to consider how far certain assertions made by the accused are in accordance with the provisions contained in the two Sub-sections of that section.

The High Court had before it a large number of writ petitions and applications under Section 482 of the Code of Criminal Procedure. Most of those petitions were filed on behalf of the accused but a few were also at the instance of the complainants. On the basis of the grievances made and reliefs prayed for in those petitions the High Court framed the following two questions as arising for its consideration.

In these appeals we are required to consider the special provisions laid down by Section 145 of the Negotiable Instruments Act, 1881 (`the Act', hereinafter) for a dishonoured cheque trial and to consider how far certain assertions made by the accused are in accordance with the provisions contained in the two Sub-sections of that section.

Held,

3. The High Court had before it a large number of writ petitions and applications under Section 482 of the Code of Criminal Procedure. Most of those petitions were filed on behalf of the accused but a few were also at the instance of the complainants. On the basis of the grievances made and reliefs prayed for in those petitions the High Court framed the following two questions as arising for its consideration:

(A) Whether Sub-section (2) of Section 145 of the Negotiable Instruments Act, 1881, (for short, "the Act") confers an unfettered right on the complainant and the accused to apply to the court seeking direction to give oral examination-in-chief of a person giving evidence on affidavit, even in respect of the facts stated therein and that if such a right is exercised, whether the court is obliged to examine such a person in spite of the mandate of Section 145(1) of the Act?

(B) Whether the provisions of Section 145 of the Act, as amended by the Negotiable Instruments (Amendment and Miscellaneous Provisions) Act, 2002, (for short "the amending Act of 2002") are applicable to the complaints under Section 138 of the Act pending on the date on which the amendment came into force? In other words, do the amended provisions of Section 145(1) and (2) of the Act operate retrospectively?

. As stated by Justice Frankfurter of the US Supreme Court (see *"Of Law and Men: Papers and addresses of Felix Frankfurter"*)

Even within their area of choice the courts are not at large. They are confined by the nature and scope of the judicial function in its particular exercise in the field of interpretation. They are under the constraints imposed by the judicial function in our democratic society. As a matter of verbal recognition certainly, no one will gainsay that the function in construing a statute is to ascertain the meaning of words used by the legislator. To go beyond it is to usurp a power which our democracy has lodged in its elected legislature. The great judges have constantly admonished there brethren of the need for discipline in observing the limitations. A judge must not rewrite a statute, neither to enlarge nor to contract it. Whatever temptations the statesmanship of policy- making might wisely suggest, construction must eschew interpolation and evisceration. He must not read in by way of creation. He must not read out except to avoid patent nonsense or internal contradiction.

In *Duport Steels Ltd. v. Sirs* [1980] 1 All ER 529, 534, Lord Scarman expounded the legal position in the following words:

But in the field of statute law the judge must be obedient to the will of Parliament as expressed in its enactments. In this field Parliament makes and unmakes the law. The judge's duty is to interpret and to apply the law not to change it to meet the judge's idea of what justice requires. Interpretation does, of course, imply in the interpreter a power of choice where differing construction are possible. But our law require the judge to choose the construction which in his judgment best meets the legislative purpose of the enactment. If the result be unjust but inevitable, the judge may say so and invite Parliament to reconsider its provision. But he must not deny the statute.

In light of the above we have no hesitation in holding that the High Court was in error in taking the view, that on a request made by the accused the magistrate may allow him to tender his evidence on affidavit and consequently, we set aside the direction as contained in sub-paragraph (r) of 34 paragraph 45 of the High Court judgment. The appeal arising from SLP (Crl.) No. 3915/2006 is allowed.

All the remaining six appeals are dismissed.

There shall be no order as to costs.

SEVENTEEN

A.C. NARAYANAN AND ORS. VS. STATE OF MAHARASHTRA AND ORS., 2015

Hon'ble Judges/Coram: S.J. Mukhopadhaya and S.A. Bobde, JJ.

Relevant Section:

Negotiable Instruments Act, 1881 - Section 138

Equivalent Citation: 2015(2)ACR1407(SC), 2015II AD (S.C.) 153, 2015(147)AIC113, AIR2015SC1198, 2015 (1) ALD(Crl.) 1031 (SC), 2015 (88) ACC 903, 2015ALLMR(Cri)781, 2015(2)ALT(Cri)SC43, 2015(1)BomCR(Cri)655, I(2015)CCR347(SC), [2015]125CLA159(SC), 2015CriLJ1434, 2015(1)Crimes116(SC), 2015(1)CTC853, 2015(3)JCC185(SC), 2015 (1) KHC 456, 2015-2-LW(Crl)607, 2015(1)N.C.C.383, 2015(1)RCR(Criminal)823, 2015(1)SCALE698, (2015)12SCC203, 2015 (2) SCJ 67, [2015]130SCL32(SC), 2015(1)UC399, 2015 (1) WLN 88 (SC), MANU/SC/0934/2015

No. of Pages in the Original Judgement: 8

Case Note:

Criminal - Recall of process - Denial thereto - High Court confirmed dismissal of applications preferred by Appellant-Accused for discharge/ recalling process against him - Hence, present appeal - Whether application for discharge/recall of process was not maintainable - Held, since complaint was not filed abiding with provisions of Act, it was not open to Magistrate to take cognizance - Even order of issue of process did not mention that

Magistrate had perused any Power of Attorney for issuing process - Magistrate wrongly took cognizance in matter and Court below erred in putting onus on Appellant rather than Complainant - Impugned order set aside - Proceedings in question against Appellant were quashed - Appeal allowed.

Criminal - Conviction - Challenge thereto - Section 138 of Negotiable Instruments Act, 1881 - High Court convicted Appellant by setting aside order passed by Metropolitan Magistrate wherein Appellant-Accused dismissed complaint filed by Respondent-Company under Section 138 of Act - Hence, present appeal - Whether impugned order rightly convicted Appellant from offence in question - Held, one employee of Company signed complaint and Deputy General Manager of Company i.e. Prosecution Witness gave evidence as if he knew everything though he did not know anything - There was nothing on record to suggest that he was authorized by Managing Director or any Director - Therefore, Magistrate rightly acquitted Appellant - Impugned order set aside - Appeal allowed

Brief facts of the case:

The accused-Appellant, A.C. Narayanan challenged the common order dated 29th November, 2000 passed by the Additional Chief Metropolitan Magistrate, 9th Court, Bandra, Mumbai (hereinafter referred to as the, 'Trial Court') by filing applications Under Section 482 of the Code of Criminal Procedure, 1973 before the High Court. By the said common order the applications preferred by the Appellant-A.C. Narayanan for discharge/ recalling process against him was rejected by the Trial Court. The High Court by impugned judgment dated 12th August, 2005, dismissed the applications preferred by the Appellant and upheld the order passed by the Trial Court.

Held,

In this case it is not in dispute that the complaint was filed by one Shri V. Shankar Prasad claiming to be General Power of Attorney of the complainant company. Subsequently PW-1 Shri Ravinder Singh gave the evidence on behalf of the Company under the General Power of Attorney given by the complainant Company. The complaint was not signed either by Managing Director or Director of the Company. It is also not in dispute that PW-1 is only the employee of the Company. As per Resolution of the Company i.e. Ex. P3 under first part Managing Director and Director are authorized to file suits and criminal complaints against the debtors for recovery of money and for prosecution. Under third part of the said

Resolution they were authorized to appoint or nominate any other person to appear on their behalf in the Court and engage lawyer etc. But nothing on the record suggest that an employee is empowered to file the complaint on behalf of the Company. This apart, Managing Director and Director are authorized persons of the Company to file the complaint by signing and by giving evidence. At best the said persons can nominate any person to represent themselves or the Company before the Court. In the present case one Shri Shankar Prasad employee of the Company signed the complaint and the Deputy General Manager of the Company i.e. PW-1 gave evidence as if he knows everything though he does not know anything. There is nothing on the record to suggest that he was authorized by the Managing Director or any Director. Therefore, Magistrate by judgment dated 30th October, 2001 rightly acquitted the Appellant. In such a situation, the case of the Appellant is fully covered by decision by the larger bench of this Court passed in the present appeal. We have no other option but to set aside the impugned judgment dated 19th September, 2007 passed by the High Court of Judicature, Andhra Pradesh at Hyderabad in Criminal Appeal No. 578 of 2002. The judgment and order dated 30th October, 2001 passed by the Court of XVIII Metropolitan Magistrate, Hyderabad in C.C. No. 18 of 2000 is upheld.

The appeals are allowed accordingly.

PPP

EIGHTEEN

A.K. SINGHANIA AND ORS. VS GUJARAT STATE FERTILIZER COMPANY LTD. AND ORS., 2013

Hon'ble Judges/Coram:C.K. Prasad and Kurian Joseph, JJ.

Relevant Section:

Negotiable Instruments Act, 1881 - Section 138

Equivalent Citation: 2013(3)ACR3030, 2013XI AD (S.C.) 1, 2013(132)AIC79, AIR2014SC71, 2014(1)ALD(Cri)317, 2014 (84) ACC 1, 2013ALLMR(Cri)4098, 2013ALLMR(Cri)4098(SC), 2014 (1) ALT (Crl.) 164 (A.P.), IV(2013)BC623, 2014(1)BomCR771, 2014(1)BomCR(Cri)411, IV(2013)CCR325(SC), [2014]118CLA172(SC), 117(2014)CLT385, [2014]182CompCas572(SC), (2013)4CompLJ486(SC), (2013)4CompLJ486(SC), 2014CriLJ340, 2013(4)Crimes421(SC), 2014(1)J.L.J.R.311, 2013(4)JCC226, JT2013(13)SC583, 2013 (4) KHC 264, 2013-2-LW(Crl)785, 2014(1)N.C.C.220, 2014(1)PLJR435, 2013(4)RCR(Civil)844, 2013(4)RCR(Criminal)777, 2013(12)SCALE673, (2013)16SCC630, [2013]9SCR1069, MANU/SC/1081/2013

No. of Pages in the Original Judgement: 5

Case Note:

Negotiable Instruments Act, 1881 - Sections 138 and 141--Dishonour of cheque--Offence by company for dishonour of cheque--Culpability of Directors to be decided with reference to Section 141--Necessary to specifically aver in complaint under Section 141 that at time offence committed, person accused was in-charge of, and responsible for conduct of business of company--No averment that two accused-appellants in instant case were in-charge of and responsible for conduct of business of company at time offence was committed--No essential averments in complaints--Prosecution of accused-appellants cannot be allowed to continue--Impugned order of High Court quashing prosecution of accused-appellants cannot be interfered with.

Brief Facts of the case:

In all these special leave petitions common question of law and facts arise and, therefore, they have been heard together and are being disposed of by this common judgment.

In all these cases we are concerned with accused A.K. Singhania and Vikram Prakash. Several complaints were filed by Gujarat State Fertilizer Company against Esslon Synthetics Ltd., its Chairman, Managing Director and other Directors including aforesaid A.K. Singhania and Vikram Prakash alleging commission of an offence under Section 138 of the Negotiable Instruments Act, hereinafter referred to as 'the Act'.

In Harshendra Kumar D. v. RebatilataKoley (2011) 3 SCC 351, after referring to its earlier decisions in S.M.S. Pharmaceuticals Ltd. (supra), National Small Industries Corpn. Ltd. (supra), N. Rangachari v. Bharat Sanchar Nigam Ltd. (2007) 5 SCC 108 and K.K. Ahuja v. V.K. Vora (2009) 10 SCC 48, this Court reiterated the same view.

We have found on fact that there is no averment that the two accused herein were in charge of and responsible for the conduct of the business of the company at the time the offence was committed. Hence, there is no essential averment in the complaints. In view of what we have observed above, the prosecution of accused A.K. Singhania and accused Vikram Prakash cannot be allowed to continue. Accordingly, the order of the High Court quashing the prosecution of the accused Vikram Prakash is not fit to be interfered with. For the same reason the order passed by the High Court declining the prayer of A.K. Singhania for quashing of the prosecution cannot be sustained and the appeals preferred by him deserve to be allowed.

In the result, we dismiss the appeals preferred by the complainant Gujarat State Fertilizers Company Ltd. and allow the appeals preferred by A.K. Singhania and quash his prosecution in all these cases.

NINETEEN

A.R. RADHA KRISHNA VS. DASARI DEEPTHI AND ORS., 2019

Hon'ble Judges/Coram:N.V. Ramana, Mohan M. Shantanagoudar and Indira Banerjee, JJ.

Relevant Section:

Negotiable Instruments Act, 1881 - Section 138, Section 141

Equivalent Citation: AIR2019SC2518, 2019 (2) ALD(Crl.) 805 (SC), 2019 (2) ALT (Crl.) 368 (A.P.), III(2019)BC412(SC), [2019]150CLA302(SC), [2019]213CompCas352(SC), (2019)4CompLJ1(SC), 2019(2)Crimes374(SC), 2019(3)Crimes181(SC), 2019GLH(1)674, 2019(2)RCR(Criminal)339, 2019(3)RLW2348(SC), (2019)15SCC550, MANU/SC/0571/2019

No. of Pages in the Original Judgement: 2

Case Note:

Criminal Matters - Matters Challenging Prosecution Under Negotiable Instruments Act

Brief Facts of the case:

These appeals, by special leave, are directed against the order dated 22.09.2017 passed by the High Court of Judicature at Hyderabad for the State of Telangana and the State of Andhra Pradesh in Criminal Petition Nos. 6508, 6530 & 6531 of 2017, whereby the High Court allowed the Criminal Petitions filed by Respondent Nos. 1 and 2 and set aside the cognizance order passed by the trial court.

The case of the prosecution in brief is that the Appellant had entered into an investment agreement with M/s. Dhruti Infra Projects Limited (accused

No. 1) on 01.12.2013 on the basis of representation of Respondent Nos. 1 and 2 herein, who were the Directors of the said Company. The Appellant invested a total amount of ` 2,11,50,000/- in the said project. According to the Appellant, as on 31.03.2016, a total amount of ` 1,81,50,000/- was left to be repaid to him along with applicable interest on it. Thereafter, upon several representations by the Appellant, M/s. Dhruti Infra Projects Limited agreed to repay the amount via issue of seven cheques in favour of the Appellant. Six cheques for ` 25,00,000/- each and one cheque for ` 30,00,000/- were drawn on different dates by the authorised signatory, i.e., M.D. of M/s. Dhruti Infra Projects Limited, which were returned dishonored, on presentation by the Appellant, with the remark "Payment stopped by Drawer".

Held,

In the above view of the matter, the instant appeals are allowed and the impugned order dated 22.09.2017, passed by the High Court of Judicature at Hyderabad for the State of Telangana and the State of Andhra Pradesh in Criminal Petition Nos. 6508, 6530 & 6531 of 2017, is set aside and that of the trial court is restored.

Before parting with the matter, we make it clear that we have not expressed any opinion on the merits of the case pending before the trial court. Needless to say, the trial court will adjudicate the matter on its own merits uninfluenced by any of the observations made herein.

However, keeping in view the nature of the case, we direct the trial court to expedite the trial and dispose of the same in accordance with law.

TWENTY

PUNJAB AND SINDH BANK VS. VINKAR SAHAKARI BANK LTD. AND ORS., 2001

Hon'ble Judges/Coram:K.T. Thomas and S.N. Variava, JJ.

Relevant Section:

Negotiable Instruments Act, 1881 - Section 138; Section 118

Equivalent Citation: 2001(3)ACR2774(SC), 2001VIIAD(SC)537, AIR2001SC3641, 2001 (43) ACC 788, 2001(4)ALLMR(SC)474, 2002(1)ALT(Cri)55, IV(2001)CCR50(SC), [2001]107CompCas208(SC), (2001)4CompLJ188(SC), (2001)4CompLJ188(SC), 2002CriLJ93, 2001GLH(3)372, JT2001(8)SC22, 2001(4)MhLJ894(SC), 2001MPLJ580(SC), 2001(4)RCR(Criminal)245, RLW2001(3)SC428, 2001(6)SCALE352, (2001)7SCC721, 2001(2)UC598, 2001(2)UJ1577MANU/SC/0567/2001

No. of Pages in the Original Judgement: 4

Case Note:

Negotiable Instruments Act, 1881 - Section 138--Pay Order-Dishonour of--Complaint under Section--High Court quashed complaint holding that the Pay Order is not a Cheque--HELD-- Dissent from High Court.

Negotiable Instruments Act, 1881 - Sections 9, 50 and 118 (g)--"Holder in due course"-- Means--Person who for consideration became possessor of cheque-- If payable to bearer before amount become payable--Until contrary is proved--Holder of negotiable instrument shall be "holder in due course"

Brief facts of the case:

This case involves a queer situation when a "Pay Order" was dishonoured by the drawer bank. The holder thereof (Punjab and Sindh Bank) filed a complaint under Section 138 of the Negotiable Instruments Act, 1881 (for short 'the Act'). The drawer bank and its officials have been arraigned as accused in the complaint. But a single Judge of the High Court of Bombay quashed the complaint mainly on the premise that the instrument (described as the "pay order") is not a cheque. The Punjab & Sindh Bank has filed this appeal in challenge of the aforesaid order of the High Court. Besides the premise stated above learned single Judge of the High Court adopted two more grounds for quashing the complaint. One among them is that even assuming that the instrument is a cheque it was crossed and hence the complainant- bank should only have collected the amount and remitted the same to the account of the person shown as payee in the instrument. The other is, the complainant was not a 'holder in due course' inasmuch as no endorsement was made on the instrument in the manner prescribed under Section 50 of the Act and hence the complainant has no locus standi to file the complaint.

The short facts leading to the filing of the complaint are these:

The first accused in the complaint is a co-operative bank. It drew the Pay Order on 18.12.1992 in a sum of Rs. 48.40 lacs, the relevant inscriptions of which are the following: "Payee's account only - To pay Punjab & Sindh Bank - M/s. Poise Leasing and Finance Company Ltd. or order". According to the appellant the said Pay Order was got assigned to the complainant-bank from M/s. Poise Leasing and Finance Company Ltd. When the instrument was presented for clearance before the first accused bank on 18.12.1992 it was returned with the remarks "funds uncleared". It was again presented on 6.1.1993 and then it was returned dishonoured with the remarks "drawer bank's funds with our bank i.e. sponsoring bank, are insufficient". This was followed by sending a notice to the first accused bank as contemplated in Section 138 of the Act. since the amount was not paid within the statutory period a complaint was filed on 9.3.1993.

Held,

The third ground for quashing the complaint is that the complainant was not "a holder in due course" in the absence of an endorsement made on the instrument in the manner prescribed under section 50 of the Act. This ground was adopted by the learned single Judge without regard to certain relevant provisions of the Act.

Section 142 of the Act envisages a complaint to be made in writing "either by the payee or the holder in due course of the cheque, as the case may be". Section 8 of the Act defines "holder" as any person entitled in his own name to the possession of the cheque and to receive or recover the amount due thereon from the parties thereto. We have no doubt that complainant-bank was well within its right to possess the cheque and to receive or recover the amount covered by the instrument. "Holder in due course" means a person who for consideration became the possessor of a cheque if payable to bearer before the amount became payable. (vide Sec. 9).

In this context reference has to be made to Section 118(g) of the Act which contains a mandate that until the contrary is proved the holder of a negotiable instrument shall be presumed to be a holder in due course. Thus there is no escape for the court from drawing such presumption.

It is undisputed that the complainant-company is the holder of the instrument on its own right. As such it could be a holder in due course also until the concerned party adduces evidence to rebut the presumption. It is of course open to the respondents to rebut the presumption in the trial but till then the High Court could not say that the complainant is not a holder in due course at all.

For the aforesaid reasons we allow this appeal and set aside the impugned judgment. The trial shall now proceed to reach the final judgment without any more delay.

Videos & Tv Shows On Law & Exim

List of some important videos & TV shows on Law & EXIM by Adv. Jayprakash Somani on his YouTube Channel 'Jayprakash Somani EXIM & Legal'

Legal Videos: Hindi -English

1) SLP in Supreme Court / Special Leave Petitions in the Supreme Court of India

2) Transfer of Civil & Criminal Cases by the Supreme Court of India / Transfer of Matrimonial Cases

3) Appellate Jurisdiction of the Supreme Court of India

4) Jurisdictions of the Supreme Court of India

5) Public Interest Litigation in the Supreme Court of India / PIL in Supreme Court

6) Article 32 Writ Petitions in the Supreme Court of India

7) Bail Matters Top 10 Supreme Court Cases

8) FIR Quashing in High Court & Supreme Court

9) Bail & Anticipatory Bail Matters in Supreme Court

10) Insolvency & Bankruptcy Matters in the Supreme Court

11) Insolvency & Bankruptcy Code 2016 Part 1

12) Insolvency & Bankruptcy Code 2016 Part 2

13) Insolvency & Bankruptcy Code 2016 Part 3

14) Corporate Liquidation Process

15) Supreme Court Rules & Procedures Webinar of 2.5 hour on Zoom

16) RDDBFI Act, 1993 (Introduction)

17) The Indian Contact Act 1872

18) Negotiable Instruments Act (Introduction)

19) How to avoid matrimonial disputes& some more videos

20)SEBI Matters in the Supreme Court

21) Matrimonial Matters: Supreme Court's 20 Case Laws

22) Consumer Matters Supreme Court's 20 Case Laws

23) Service Matters Supreme Court's 20 Case Laws

24) How to Search Lawyer for Your Matter

25) Property Matters Supreme Court's 20 Case Laws

26) Bail Matters: Supreme Court's 20 Case Laws

27) Supreme Court / High Court Vacation Benches

28)69000 Teacher's Recruitment Matters of UP Government in the Supreme Court

29) Contempt of Court Matters in the Supreme Court

30) Advocate Act's Matters in the Supreme Court

31) Business Law Matters in the Supreme Court

32) Banking Matters in the Supreme Court

33) Labour Law Matters in the Supreme Court

34) Arbitration Matters in the Supreme Court

35) Careers in Law -Zoom Webinar by Adv. Jayprakash Somani

36) Civil Matters in the Supreme Court

37) Consumer Protection Act | Consumer Matters in the Supreme Court

38) Corporate Matters in the Supreme Court

39) Criminal Matters in the Supreme Court

40) Role of Respondent in the Supreme Court of India

41) Motor Vehicle Accident Matters in Supreme Court with case laws

42) Article 131 Original Suits in Supreme Court

43)PIL in Supreme Court/ Public Interest Litigations in the Supreme Court of India'

44)CAB Citizenship Amendment Bill is not Unconstitutional

45) Supreme Court of India Cases & Process – Marathi

46) Legal Services Export / Export of Legal Services

47) Transfer of Matrimonial Cases by the Supreme Court of India

48) Public Interest Litigation PIL

49) The Specific Relief Act (Introduction)

50) Corporate Insolvency Resolution Process CIRP

51)ABMM's Career 5 - Careers in Law

52) Transfer of cases by Supreme Court

53) Writ Petitions in High Court & Supreme Court of India

54) Supreme Court Jurisdictions - Appeals, SLP, Writ Petitions, Transfer, Original, Review, Curative

55)LEGAL INDIA TV Show: Cases Handled in Supreme Court

56) Corporate Liquidation Process

57) Legal Services Export / Export of Legal Services

EXIM Videos: Hindi -English

1) Yes, I can do Import Export Business Easily! 36 points excellent video in Hindi

2) Yes, I can do Import Export Business Easily! 36 points excellent video in English

3) Import Export Business – Hindi video

4) Import Export Business - English video

5) Export Import Marathi TV Interview

6) Scope for Commerce Students in International Business- TV Show

7) Scope for Management Student in International Business- TV Show

8) Scope for Engineering Students in International Business – TV Show

9) Women in International Business- TV Show

10) How to do Import Export Business Successfully!'

11) Where one can get full information on Import Export Business?

12) What to do import & export?

13) Import Export Workshop/ Training/Course/ Diploma

14) How to Start Import Export Business & How to grow it. Live Webinar

15) Success Stories & Failure Stories in Import & Export Business

16) For MSME Scope in Export & Import...

17) Exports In Agri. & Food Products – English & some more videos

18) Exports to Dubai, Aabudhabii. e. UAE

19) Jewellery Exports from India

20) How to attend EXIM workshop to become excellent Exporter

21) Import Export Best Training Course – Online & Offline

22) Agri Product Export

23) Scope for Woman in International Business

24) Management Graduates Scope in International Business

25) Pharma Product's Export

26) Best Import Export Course | Practical Training | Aaronica Global Exim

27) Import Export Business for Commerce Graduates

28) How Do I Get Export Orders? Finding International Buyers

29) What Is APEDA In Import Export Business?

30) Which Is The Best Product To Export From India?

31)EXIM Remark by Manoj Kumar Faridabad

32)EXIM Remarks by Mahesh Telangana

33) What Licenses I Need To Start Import/ Export?

34) How Can I Increase My Import Export Business?

35) Which Is Best B2B Website For Import/Export Business?

36) Export Import Management with Global Marketing

37) How to Start Export Import Business | 51 Points Video

38) Scope for Commerce & Other Graduates in International Business
39)BE A SUCCESSFUL EXPORTER FOR OUR NATION - Marathi video
40) Export of Textile , Cotton, Agri., Food, & other products & services
41) Exports from MP, CG, MH, GJ & CA in Fresh Fruits & Vegetables
42) Exports in Agri. & Food Products- Hindi
43) Start your Online/E-Commerce Business
44) How to Start Export Import Business & Grow it
45) Exports in Textile & Other Products
46) Start and grow EXIM business - Live English Webinar
47)'Import Export Business!' Why, Who, What & How can one do it easily!!
48) Live: Export of Product & Services During & After Lock Down Period
49) Frauds in Import Export Business
50) Import Export for Business Man
51) Import & Export for Women
51) Import & Export for Graduate & Post - Graduate Students
52) Agriculture Exports from India
53) Digital Marketing Setup - Marathi
54)2nd Secret of Successful Businessman
55) Digital Marketing Set up
56) Legal Services Export / Export of Legal Services
57) Export & Import with UAE
58) Service Exports / Exports by Service Providers
59) Import Export Workshop/ Training/Course/ Diploma
60) Exports & Imports with USA
61) Selection on Product for Export
62) Top Products Exported from India
63) What to do import & export?
64)ABMM Career 2 - 'Careers in Business & Industries
65) How to do Import Export Business Successfully!'
66)5 Secrets of Successful Businessman
67) Export from MP, Chhattisgarh & Vidarbha Nagpur
68)EXIM Hindi - Textile & Apparel Export
69)EXIM Hindi - Export Import Practical Training In Delhi, Kolkata, Mumbai and Pune
70) Import Export Business
71) Import Export Business Hindi
72) Import Export Business English video

73) Import Export Business Marathi

74) Women in International Business by Exim Guru Adv. Jayprakash Somani

75) Opportunities in Foreign Trade- Adv. Jayprakash Somani's special interview

List Of Adv. Jayprakash Somani's Books

1. Supreme Court of India's Leading Case Laws on 'Insolvency & Bankruptcy Code 2016'
2. Bail Matters – Supreme Court's Latest Leading Case Laws
3. Arbitration Matters- Supreme Court's Latest Leading Case Laws
4. Property Matters - Supreme Court's Latest Leading Case Laws
5. Matrimonial Matters- Supreme Court's Latest Leading Case Laws
6. Election Matters- Supreme Court's Latest Leading Case Laws
7.SEBI Matters- Supreme Court's Latest Leading Case Laws
8. Banking Matters- Supreme Court's Latest Leading Case Laws
9. Service Matters- Supreme Court's Latest Leading Case Laws
10. Contempt of Court Matters- Supreme Court's Latest Leading Case Laws
11. Consumer Protection Matters- Supreme Court's Latest Leading Case Laws
12. Corporate Law- Supreme Court's Latest Leading Case Laws
13. Supreme Court's AOR Exam- Leading Cases
14. Armed Force Tribunal - Supreme Court's Latest Leading Case Laws
15. Acquittal From 376 - Supreme Court's Latest Leading Case Laws
16. Negotiable Instrument Act– Supreme Court's Latest Leading Case Laws
17. Contract Act- Supreme Court's Latest Leading Case Laws
18. Insider trading- Supreme Court's Latest Leading Case Laws
19. Foreign Exchange and Management Act- Supreme Court's Latest Leading Case Laws
20. Income Tax Act- Supreme Court's Latest Leading Case Laws
21. Company Law- Supreme Court's Latest Leading Case Laws
22. Competition & Monopoly Matters- Supreme Court's Latest Leading Case Laws
23. Compassionate Appointment- Service Matters- Supreme Court's Latest Leading Case Laws
24. Compulsory Retirement- Service Matters- Supreme Court's Latest Leading Case Laws
25. Voluntary Retirement- Service Matters- Supreme Court's Latest Leading Case Laws

26. Removal/Dismissal/Termination from Service- Supreme Court's Latest Leading Case Laws

27. Seniority- Service Matter- Supreme Court's Latest Leading Case Laws

28. Promotion- Service Matter- Supreme Court's Latest Leading Case Laws

29. Equal Pay for Equal Work- Service Matter- Supreme Court's Latest Leading Case Laws

30. Condition of Service- Service Matter- Supreme Court's Latest Leading Case Laws

31. Customs Act- Supreme Court's Leading Case Laws

32. Information Technology Act- Supreme Court's Latest Leading Case Laws

These Books are available online at

1. **Notion Press:** https://notionpress.com/author/jayprakash_somani
2. **Amazon:** https://www.amazon.in/s?k=jayprakash+somani
3. **Flipkart:** https://www.flipkart.com/search?q=Jayprakash%20Somani

PPP

9 798886 298901

Printed by Libri Plureos GmbH in Hamburg,
Germany